Yo-Ho-Ha-Ha-Ha!

A Pirate Joke Book

Stephen Hillenburg

Based on the TV series *SpongeBob SquarePants®* created by Stephen
Hillenburg as seen on Nickelodeon®

ISBN-13: 978-0-439-92241-8
ISBN-10: 0-439-92241-0

12 11 10 9 8 7 6 5 4 3 2 1   7 8 9 10 11 12/0

Printed in the U.S.A.

First Scholastic printing, January 2007

NICKELODEON

SpongeBob SquarePants

Yo-Ho-Ha-Ha-Ha!

A Pirate Joke Book

by David Lewman

SCHOLASTIC INC.

New York Toronto London Auckland Sydney
Mexico City New Delhi Hong Kong Buenos Aires

What did the pirates do when SpongeBob asked to join them?

They welcomed him with open ahrrs.

Ahrr!

Ahrr!

Ahrr!

Pearl: Who steers the ship while the captain naps?

Sandy: His co-pirate.

Ahrr!

4

Who helped SpongeBob find his missing treasure?

A pirate detective.

Ahrr!

Patrick: What's a pirate's favorite holiday?

SpongeBob: Ahrrbor Day.

Ahrr!

Ahrr!

Mrs. Puff: Which pirate is the most musical?

Mr. Krabs: Sing-along John Silver.

Squidward: Which pirate is the sleepiest?

Patrick: Long Yawn Silver.

Patrick: Why did the pirate go up in a hot-air balloon?

Squidward: He heard every cloud has a silver lining.

Pearl: Which pirate is the messiest?

SpongeBob: Long John Spiller.

Squidward: Which pirate loves to eat?

SpongeBob: Snackbeard.

Squidward: Why did the pirate send her sword to school?

Sandy: She wanted it to be sharp.

Sandy: What's the difference between a pirate present and a runaway pumpkin?

Squidward: One's a gift sword, and the other's a swift gourd.

Pearl: Why did the pirate cut off his beard when the clouds rolled in?

SpongeBob: He was shaving it for a rainy day.

Why was the Flying Dutchman looking for clues?

He was on a treasure haunt.

Mr. Krabs: What's a pirate's favorite state?

Sandy: Ahrrkansas.

SpongeBob: What's a pirate's favorite sport?

Patrick: Ahrrchery.

Mr. Krabs: Why did the bug crawl up the pirate's sword?

Plankton: It wanted to get to the point.

Squidward: What is a pirate's favorite nut?

Sandy: The chestnut.

Patrick: How do pirates find buried chests without a map?

SpongeBob: They go on a treasure hunch.

Mr. Krabs: Knock-knock.

SpongeBob: Who's there?

Mr. Krabs: Sherlock.

SpongeBob: Sherlock who?

Mr. Krabs: Sure, lock the chest—it's full of treasure!

Sandy: Did the pirate really open the locked chest just by singing a song?

Patrick: Yes, she sang in the right key.

Squidward: What did the pirates do to the electric eel?

Plankton: They made him shock the plank.

Mr. Krabs: How did the pirate clean the golden floor?

SpongeBob: With a treasure mop.

Patrick: Why do pirate flags wave?

SpongeBob: To say hello!

SpongeBob: Why are pirate flags always grouchy?

Sandy: Because they have *crossbones*.

15

Mrs. Puff: Who wears an eye patch, a wooden leg, and a chest protector?

SpongeBob: An umpirate.

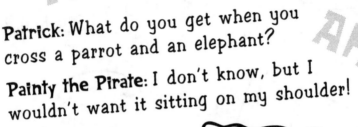

Ahrr!

Patrick: What do you get when you cross a parrot and an elephant?

Ahrr!

Painty the Pirate: I don't know, but I wouldn't want it sitting on my shoulder!

Ahrr!

SpongeBob: What kind of jokes do parrots tell?

Mr. Krabs: Squawk-squawk jokes.

Ahrr!

SNAP!

Ahrr!

Ahrr!

SpongeBob: What do parrots use to wake up in the morning?

Squidward: An alarm squawk.

Ahrr!

Patrick: What's a pirate's favorite animal?

Sandy: The ahrrmadillo!

SpongeBob: What's a pirate's favorite vegetable?

Squidward: The ahrrtichoke!

Patchy the Pirate: What did the pirate name his wooden-legged horse?

Painty the Pirate: Peg-asus!

Sandy: Why was the parrot mad at the pirate?

Pearl: Because he gave her the cold shoulder.

SpongeBob: Did the parrot study for his flying exam?

Mrs. Puff: No, he just winged it.

Patrick: Did the old parrot help the young parrot?

SpongeBob: Yes, he took him under his wing.

SpongeBob: Who wears an eye patch, says "ahrrr," and hunts for fossils?

Squidward: An ahrrchaeologist!

Squidward: What's a parrot's favorite holiday?

Plankton: Feather's Day.

Why is Painty the Pirate stuck in a frame?

He's a work of ahrrt.

SpongeBob: Why did the pirate tie a piece of fruit to his face?

Mr. Krabs: He wanted to wear an eye peach.

SpongeBob: Where do pirates play pinball?

Patrick: The ahrrcade!

SpongeBob: What's a pirate's best basketball move?

Patrick: His hook shot.

Squidward: Who designs pirates' houses?

Mr. Krabs: Ahrrchitects!

Patrick: What kind of bees do pirates like?

Mr. Krabs: Rubies!

Sandy: What is a pirate's favorite fish?

SpongeBob: The goldfish.

SpongeBob: Why does the pirate go to the jeweler every year?

Squidward: To have his earring tested.

Why did Painty the Pirate stop talking to Patchy the Pirate?

They had a big ahrrgument.

Ahrr!

Ahrr!

Ahrr!

Plankton: Which ocean is the pirate's favorite?

SpongeBob: The Ahrrctic Ocean.

Squidward: What's a pirate's best boxing punch?

Plankton: A right hook.

Is Painty the Pirate guilty of bad singing?

No, he was framed.

Patrick: Why do monkeys climb on pirates?

SpongeBob: To steal their bandanas.

When Patchy the Pirate's parrot got grouchy, why did Patrick try to eat him?

He'd heard he was a crabby Potty.

SpongeBob: What do pirate ships wear to look scary?

Squidward: Halloween masts.

SpongeBob: What bird is the pirate's favorite?

Sandy: The goldfinch.

Patrick: Where do pirates keep their eggs?

Mr. Krabs: In the crow's nest.

SpongeBob: Which part of a pirate ship is the smelliest?

Patrick: The poop deck.

Which part of a pirate ship is Mr. Krabs's favorite?

The quarterdeck.

Squidward: What dive do pirates like to do?

Patrick: The cannonball!

Was SpongeBob ready to be shot out of the pirates' cannon?

Yes, he was really on the ball.

Plankton: What did the big cannon say at the celebration?

Mr. Krabs: "Business is booming!"

Patchy the Pirate: What's the difference between a ghost and a cannon?

Painty the Pirate: One likes to *boo* and the other likes to *boom.*

Did Patrick do a good job of loading the cannon?

No, he dropped the ball.

Why did Patrick try to play music on the crate the cannon came in?

He'd heard it was a boom box.

Squidward: What happened when the cannon asked the pirates to stop using him?

Mr. Krabs: He was fired.

Patrick: What game do cannons like to play?

Plankton: Fuseball.

Sandy: Did the cannon have fun on his birthday?

SpongeBob: Yes, he had a blast!

What did the angry pirate do when Patrick accidentally lit the cannon?

He blew a fuse.

Patrick: What do pirates use to keep their boots on?

Sandy: Swashbuckles.

SpongeBob: How did the pirate do on his boating test?

Mrs. Puff: He sailed through it.

Mrs. Puff: Why did the pirates spread their wares out on the deck?

Mr. Krabs: They were holding a garage sail.

SpongeBob: Which pirate has a big beard, a gold earring, and six legs?

Patrick: Captain Squidward.

Why did Patrick kneel down and put his palms on the pirate boat?

Someone yelled, "All hands on deck!"

Why did SpongeBob dig for treasure under the chicken coop?

He heard that *eggs* mark the spot.

Painty the Pirate: Why did the anchor stop trying to reach the sea floor?

Patchy the Pirate: He was at the end of his rope.

SpongeBob: Was the pirate wrong to forget to pack any rope?

Mr. Krabs: Yes, he was way out of line.

Ahrr!

Ahrr!

Ahrr!

Sandy: Why did the pirate climb into the ship's rigging with a book?

Squidward: He wanted to read between the lines.

Ahrr!

Ahrr!

SpongeBob: What do pirates wear under their pants?

Patrick: Their plunderwear.

Ahrr!

Ahrr!

Patrick: What did the angry pirate do when he found out his ship was overloaded?

Squidward: He went through the reef.

Squidward: What do you call four pirate ships that sink in the same spot?

Mrs. Puff: A wreck-tangle.

Mrs. Puff: Why did the pirate make his crew study?

SpongeBob: He was hoping for a scholarship.

43

Why did SpongeBob smack his ship's floor?

He thought the pirate told him to swat the deck.

Sandy: Why do pirates like to play baseball?

Plankton: They love to steal bases.

Patrick: What would Santa Claus say if he was a pirate?

Squidward: "Yo-ho-ho-ho!"

SpongeBob: What do pirates do when they can't sleep?

Mr. Krabs: Count ships.

Sandy: When is a pirate like a bird?
Plankton: When he's a-robbin'.

SpongeBob: What is the pirate's favorite bedtime story?

Patrick: "Sleeping Booty."

Shiver me timbers!

We're at the end of the book!